The Obedient Disciple

Victoria Neville

I dedicate this book to my children and my sister Bella and in memory of my sister Henrietta and my beloved father.

Table of Contents

Foreword

I feel very privileged to have been asked to write this foreword for Victoria's latest book. I have been in church leadership for 30 years and have had lots of different experiences of traditional and contemporary church, conservative and charismatic, orthodox and the progressive. I found myself in the Church of England as a Vicar and admit to finding it very challenging and sometimes a little dry. I met Victoria as she is part of a group of Christians that began meeting to pray and worship together in my parish, while exploring what God was calling us to do for His Kingdom.

Victoria stands out as someone with a deep and meaningful faith. It is a faith that she is passionate about and that I find refreshing. She has written in such a way that it gripped me and excited me, seeing what God can do through mere humans who are open to him working in their lives. Having personally experienced healing through her ministry I am convinced that God uses Victoria in a powerful way, to reveal His Kingdom through signs and wonders. As you will discover from this book Victoria came to a real faith in Jesus ten years ago and responded to God's call to renewal following a difficult period in her life. It seems that is often how God grabs hold of us. Victoria's life has been transformed by her encounter with Jesus.

Victoria writes from the heart about seven key areas in a believer's life which help each of us to experience the fullness that God has in store for us if we are truly open to allowing God to lead us by His Holy Spirit. Packed solid with personal illustrations and stories from her own journey, this book encourages us to reach out and grab hold of all that God has in store for us. She is honest about her struggles and the challenges she has faced, which encourages me to strive forward and go deeper with God. Her writing is as contagious, as Victoria is passionate and engaging. Even if you are not looking for a boost to your faith, you will find in these words penned by this reluctant writer and obedient disciple a refreshment which naturally and gently moves you into a greater excitement about what is possible with

God.

Be encouraged and amazed!

Rev'd Geoff Mumford
Vicar of the ABC Churches, York.

I highly recommend this powerful little book written by my friend Victoria Neville who is on the team of the Filling Station. If you have been saved for 40 years or you are seeking God and have big questions about where he is in the midst of pain and depression and if he's even real – then this is for you!

It is massively encouraging, faith-building and mind-blowing what stunning miracles only Jesus can do. Victoria has seen these things first-hand, and this is her testimony.

She has a child-like faith and has laid her life down for Jesus; having had a miserable childhood and a painful divorce. She loves Jesus and is used by Him powerfully in healings and deliverances – all for the glory of God. It is a spiritual pick me up and a rallying call for us to pray and see a generation turn back to God.

Kirstie Wainwright
Leader of the Cheshire Filling Station.

The growth in Victoria's faith is evident in her writing. Her faith-experience is growing wide and this comes due to her exercising in the gifts of the Spirit; experiences in healing, speaking in tongues, and the words of wisdom and knowledge. I can see Victoria becoming mighty in the use of the gift of prophecy.

I had the pleasure and the honour of instructing Victoria in a Sermon Research and Creation course, and she was my best student. As her scriptural knowledge increased, her ability to employ the Holy Scriptures very efficiently in her sermons, and in her preaching was a wonder to behold. And now, here she is a twice published author!

Victoria's heart to obey the Lord's Great Commission has led to a calling that is reaching the UK, and different parts of the world through Zoom.

It is assured that Jesus will say to Victoria one day, "Well done my good and faithful servant!"

It has also been my privilege to worship, to minister, and to serve with her for these years we have known each other.

Rev. Thomas Lewis Griffith
New Life in Christ Church, Harrogate, UK

Disclaimer

All names in this book have been changed. A grateful thanks to Jane and Reece, who have submitted their own testimonies to be used in this book and to Rev Geoff Mumford, Rev Thomas Griffith, Kirstie Wainwright, Laura Brett, Michelle Beckett, Tim and Irene Banfield and Peter Munns for all their support and encouragement.

Introduction

"You have the pen of a ready writer. There is more for you to write..."

I was not called to be a writer. When I was at school, I passed my English O-level language and literature but not with distinction. Nonetheless I have always had a love for English literature and studied both English literature and French for A level and at degree level. I achieved a BA (Hons) 2:2 in English and French at the end of my studies, as my French was definitely not as strong as my ability to write essays on English Literature. So, because I had gained a 2:2 and not a 2:1 or a first, I immediately gave up all thoughts of writing and, therefore, any occupation that involved writing, such as journalism and the like. So, at no stage have I ever thought that I would have the capability or the ability to write, least of all a book.

However, I was convicted by the Holy Spirit in September 2022 that I should start writing because of two prophetic words that were spoken over me in August 2020. Some of you will have read my first book, which was published this year in June 2023, called 'The Reluctant Disciple'. That book is really my testimony of how I was healed from depression after a miserable childhood and divorce and how I was then set on the path of evangelism and ministry. I have served on the ministry team for an international ministry for the last four years, and I serve on the team for a local ministry called the Filling Station. My book contains many testimonies of healings that I have witnessed first-hand, either on the streets or in ministry meetings.

It was birthed from a word of knowledge spoken over me at a friend's house in Harrogate. On Sundays, I would quite often go and have lunch with a lovely lady called Rosemary, who was much older than me but who used to hold gatherings in her house where we would have lunch and share Holy Communion together afterwards. In late summer 2020, on a lovely sunny day, an Irish lady walked through the door called Catherine, who had the gift of prophecy and she suddenly started speaking words of knowledge over all of us. When she got to me, she suddenly became very serious and said, "Victoria, you are to sit down, be quiet, listen and write..."

I am rather ashamed to say I did not take this word of knowledge seriously and forgot all about it until a year later I went to a service a long way north from where I live to hear an Assemblies of God preacher from America preach who also had the gift of prophecy. At the end of the service, the entire congregation went forward eager to hear what the pastor had to say, and when he reached me, he very clearly said the words, "I can see you writing a book, but I think it will be a child's book..."

Again, I was a bit non-plussed by this word of knowledge as I couldn't understand why he would say this to me when, as far as I was concerned, writing was not my forte. I did understand that it was a prophetic word but thought he was absolutely mistaken until September of 2022 when I was sitting at home reading an online Christian blog called His Kingdom Prophecy, and it clearly stated:

"Everyone has a story to tell...What's your story?"

All of a sudden, I knew without a shadow of a doubt that there was a calling on my life to write, to write down the experiences I had had on the streets praying for the homeless and the healings and baptisms in the Holy Spirit I had witnessed in ministry since 2019. So, in the autumn of 2022, I sat down and wrote for 3 weeks. The result is my first book, "The Reluctant Disciple" which was published by Kingdom Publishers in June 2023. That book would absolutely not have been written if Catherine had not been obedient and spoken that word of prophecy over me in 2019. For my part, I thought that would be it. I had been obedient and written my book, and there would be no more for me to write. God has a way of letting you know though, when your job is not finished and that he expects more. On 19 November last year, a friend of mine called me and said, "Victoria, what are you up to tomorrow? Shall we go together to Hollybush Christian Fellowship tomorrow as I haven't been for ages and I would like to go?"

Little did my friend know that I had been thinking of going there for weeks as I had been baptised in the River Ure at Hollybush ten years earlier, and I wanted to go back and tell them I had written and published a book. So, I picked my friend up on a lovely autumnal Sunday afternoon in early December and drove us up to Hollybush. The preaching I remember was very good as it was all about Elijah being caught up to heaven and how we need to be ready for the rapture of the church and fill our lamps with oil. After the service was over, the most extraordinary thing happened. I was standing in a queue for prayer when a lady suddenly made a beeline for me out of nowhere, and spoke the following words over me, "Excuse me, I don't know your name, but I have a message for you.... You have the pen of a ready writer, and there is more for you to write!"

I was dumbfounded as I really wasn't expecting this to happen. I had simply come to Hollybush just to say hello and tell them that I had written a book. I absolutely was not expecting a complete stranger to speak another prophetic word over me. But then again, I should not have been surprised because the Holy Spirit definitely moves at Hollybush. My village church is very traditional, so it was impossible for this to have happened there and so it had to happen at Hollybush as it is more charismatic and open to words of knowledge being spoken over the congregation.

I learnt that day that the Lord will get a message to you if he wants to because he is omnipresent and omniscient, and he will make a way. I had just experienced the prophetic word in action, and been shown first-hand that prophecy never comes by the will of man but by a move of the Holy Spirit'.[1] I had just witnessed the scripture come to pass, that in the last days, the Holy Spirit will be poured out upon us all ; our sons and our daughters shall prophesy.[2] So often we don't realise it, but the Lord very much still speaks to us today. The testimony of Jesus is the spirit of prophecy, and I will endeavour to show in this book how he still speaks to us clearly in 2023, just as he did in days of old. So many because of the trauma of the last few years with the recent pandemic, the lockdowns and the rollout of the recent global inoculations, are seeking answers. In this book I will try to demonstrate that Jesus is the true light that shines in the darkness, and he is the vanquisher of evil. He is the way, the truth, and the life, our only path to salvation. He is the rock that can be relied upon completely and utterly to help and protect us in this very unstable world we live in.

---

[1] 2 Peter 1:21
[2] Joel 2:28

Chapter One

Dreams And Visions

"Draw nigh, shoes off thy feet in silent awe and adoration. Draw nigh as Moses drew nigh to the burning bush."[3]

As I sit here on a freezing cold day, putting pen to paper, I am reflecting rather nostalgically that it is a year ago since my wonderfully hot and deeply memorable holiday to Israel. In November 2022 I booked myself rather last minute on a study tour of Israel for two weeks. I had never visited Israel before; for me, it was the holiday of a lifetime. When you arrive in Israel, it says you will never be the same

---

[3] God Calling: A Devotional Diary by A J Russel

again, and indeed, I was astounded to see the beauty of Israel. I dipped my toes in the Lake of Galilee, bathed in the Dead Sea, visited the north of Israel and went up to the top of Mount Carmel, where Elijah set to and massacred the prophets of Baal. We went inland to the Judean desert where David hid from Saul in the mountains at Engedi and visited the caves where the Dead Sea Scrolls were discovered at Qumran. I visited Capernaum, where Jesus preached in the synagogue and healed the paralytic man who was lowered down through the roof. We then visited Jerusalem, the Wailing Wall and important holy sites such as the church of the Holy Sepulchre and the Garden Tomb, where Jesus is thought to have been buried. I have always enjoyed reading the bible, but in Israel, it came to life in a way that it had never done before, now that I have followed in the footsteps of Jesus during his three-year ministry.

However, it was visiting the Fountain of Tears at Arad in the Judean desert, which was built as a memorial for the Jewish holocaust, that I was literally undone. A young Canadian, Rick Wienecke, obeyed a call on his life to go to Israel in 1977 and become a sculptor. Once there, he received visions of life-size statues of Jesus that he was to sculpt and of bronze statues of the Holocaust victims that he was to portray

8

underneath. He was also instructed by the Holy Spirit to build walls with water running down on either side to represent the tears of Jesus and the holocaust victims. On our visit to the museum, we were told that Rick clearly heard the Holy Spirit say to him that this memorial was to honour all those Jews who had lost their lives in the Holocaust and that Jesus wanted justice. It took Rick years to build this memorial, but he has done it in obedience and once completed, he then went to build another identical memorial outside the gates of Auschwitz. Today, many Jews are coming to Christ as a result of visiting this memorial in Arad.

Sometimes art can speak louder than words, and his memorial is an outstanding example of this. And clearly shows Jesus's immense love for the Jewish people that he would call a Canadian man to move to Israel and build the most spectacular memorial in the middle of the Judean desert to honour all those who lost their lives in the Holocaust. Rick has written a book about his life and the construction of this magnificent work of art called 'Seeds in the Wind.'

God also speaks to people very much through dreams at night; the bible is littered with dreams throughout the Old and the New Testament. The most famous example which we all know is Joseph. Joseph would have divorced Mary when he found out she was pregnant, but God sent an angel to him in a dream to tell him that the pregnancy was of God, so he went ahead with the marriage. After Jesus was born, God sent Joseph another dream to tell him that he needed to get up immediately in the middle of the night and escape to Egypt to avoid King Herod, who was intent on killing baby Jesus, in fact, Jesus had a very narrow escape, not long after Joseph, Mary and little Jesus's hurried departure, Herod's soldiers killed every single child under the age of 2 in Israel. Joseph wisely listened to this warning from the Lord and escaped in the middle of the night and took his family to safety. Then after Herod's death, God sent Joseph another dream, informing him that it was now safe for him to return home.

Years later, after Jesus's arrest and during his sentencing by Pilate, Pilate's wife received a dream from the Lord that Jesus was innocent.[4] She sent a message to warn her husband not to crucify him, but Pilate ignored her warning because of the immense pressure he was under from the Pharisees and because he wanted to keep peace in Jerusalem. After the crucifixion of Jesus, we learn that Paul receives a

---

4 Matthew 27:19

dream from the Lord depicting a man from Macedonia begging for help, so he decides to go and preach there as a result of the dream.[5]

There are also many examples of God speaking to people in dreams at night in the Old Testament. King Abimelech is warned by a dream not to touch Sarah, Abraham's wife, warning him that she was a married woman and that he would be committing adultery if he did so.[6] Joseph is rescued from prison and made Governor of Egypt in charge of the whole royal household as he had the gift of interpreting dreams. He was given the correct interpretation from the Lord of Pharaoh's dream about the 7 fat cows and the 7 lean cows, which meant that famine was coming to the land for 7 years, and Pharoah was so delighted that he put him in charge of all his affairs.[7] Jacob had a dream of a ladder going up to heaven with angels ascending and descending the ladder. He was so astonished at his encounter with God when God spoke to him and assured him that he would be with him wherever he went and would provide for him that he called the place Bethel, which means "house of

---

[5] Acts 16:16
[6] Genesis 20:3
[7] Genesis 41:1-4

11

God," and built an altar there.[8]

For me though, the most amazing dream in the Old Testament is King Nebuchadnezzar's dream of a huge statue with a gold head, silver chest and arms, stomach and thighs of bronze, legs of iron and feet which are part iron and part clay.[9] A rock is cut out, not by human hands, which strikes the statue on its feet and smashes the rest of the statue to pieces. The rock that strikes the statue becomes a huge mountain and then fills the whole earth. There is great prophetic significance to this dream. The four kingdoms are four empires that have been and gone, namely the empires of Babylon, Medo-Persia, Greece and Rome. The dream prophesies that the Kingdom of God, represented by the stone, will be set up by God in the end times, which we are now in after the Second Coming of Christ. There are too many dreams for me to write them all down, but I hope you can see that God has always communicated with his people through dreams and visions through the ages, and he still does so very much in our day. Indeed, it was reported on the news several months ago that in one night, Jesus appeared to 200 Palestinian men in Gaza

---

[8] Genesis 28:12

[9] Daniel 2:31-35

in their dreams and they all had the same dream. They all discovered that they had had the same dream on the same night and realised that it was Jesus, or Isa as they call him, that had appeared to them.

I tend not to dream very much, but I did receive a dream from the Lord in June 2023, which was all about heaven and showed me the heavenly home awaiting all those who believe in him. In my dream, I dreamt I was living in a big city in an apartment block with my sister, and I said to my sister I wanted to move house as I didn't feel safe living there. She told me that I would need to give her the keys back and that I would need a new set of keys. The scene then changed, and I found myself walking through a field filled with flowers and butterflies, but the colours were iridescent and heavenly. I had a knowing that this field was in heaven because I had two gold keys in my hand, one of which signified faith and the other key signified repentance. I also saw a beautiful cottage at the end of the field in the distance, and I knew my mother lived in the cottage. My mother died and went to be with the Lord five years ago, so I knew this dream was from the Lord as it was showing me that my future destination is heaven and that I will indeed see my mother again. Jesus reassures us of our heavenly homes in his word and tells us not to be anxious, as he has heavenly houses for us in heaven.[10] He then goes on to promise that he will come back again and rescue his bride in the rapture of the church. Dreams are one way, therefore, that the Holy Spirit speaks to us and are important. They can be warning dreams which should not be dismissed and should be taken seriously. They can also be reassuring dreams like the one I was given of seeing my mother again in heaven. Jesus does have beautiful new homes for us in heaven and my dream confirmed this!

---

[10] John 14:1-4

Chapter Two

Healing

"So fainting and needy by the lakeside of life, know that I will supply your need, not grudgingly but in full measure."[11]

Another way that Jesus reveals himself to us today is through healing. Jesus, of course, spent 3 years traveling through Israel, healing the sick, the lame and the demonised as he is the Son of God and was sent to Earth to reverse the curse of sin and death inflicted on the world due to Adam and Eve's disobedience. He is the second Adam and therefore, was commissioned by God to heal the sick everywhere

---

[11] God Calling: A Devotional Diary by A J Russel

he went and to redeem the ENTIRE WORLD from their sins by dying on the cross. There is a divine exchange that takes place on the cross where his blood atones for our sins, not just for all those alive in his day but for all generations to come until the Second Coming of Christ. All we need to do is repent of our sins and accept Jesus as our Lord and Saviour and our sins are immediately forgiven due to the atoning sacrifice of Jesus on the cross. The innocent blood that he shed on the cross paid the price for every single one of us to be forgiven if we repent and accept him as our Lord and Saviour, thereby enabling us to go to heaven when we die, as Jesus carries eternal life. He is the way, the truth and the life, and there is no other route to heaven except through him. What a truly glorious thing he did for mankind that day when he agreed to die on the cross for us when he was completely innocent of any sin or transgressions whatsoever.

When I was at school, I was very firmly taught that all the healings and miracles stopped with the death of the apostles and still today, people have shared this belief with me when I have been out witnessing on the streets. However, Jesus's heart has always been to heal the sick, which hasn't changed even in 2024. I will never forget the first time I ever went out on the streets when a young man was healed of a broken cruciate ligament by the power of God after Christa, and I prayed for him outside York Hospital. You see, Jesus is the same, yesterday, today and forever. He longs to heal the sick and is waiting for us to step out and give him the opportunity to do so.

The way we pray is absolutely crucial. Intercessory prayer, which we are used to offer up in church is very valuable, but Jesus taught his disciples to use command prayers and to always pray in the name of Jesus. Intercessory prayers are no good when someone is standing in front of you with a fractured wrist. We have to stand on the authority that Jesus has given us, know who we are in Jesus and say, "Fractured wrist, be healed in the name of Jesus," as if we are speaking directly to the body part. Intercessory prayers are important when a loved one is in hospital, but it is far more effective to put your hand on the part of the body that is sick and command it to be healed in the name of Jesus. There needs to be a paradigm shift in the way in which we pray for the sick if we want to see more revival, more healings, and creative miracles take place. In order for this to happen, we need to follow the method Jesus taught his disciples, which is to lay hands on the sick and command healing in the name of Jesus.

I don't go out evangelising now as often as I used to, but I did witness a creative miracle when I was out witnessing on the streets with a friend in Harrogate in late January 2022. We met two homeless men and got chatting to them. My friend was evangelising the man to the left of me, and so I turned and started talking to his friend, who I will call Kevin. I looked down and suddenly noticed that he had a brace on his wrist. So, I asked him what had happened, and he replied that he had fallen over recently when he had been drunk and had fractured his wrist as a result. This was too much for me, and I couldn't resist the temptation to ask if I could pray for healing for his wrist as he was on a waiting list for surgery, and the brace he had been given had an iron bar underneath, which meant he had to keep his wrist straight at all times. He was also in quite a bit of pain too. He graciously said yes and so I prayed quickly, commanding all the broken bones in his wrist to be healed and to go back into place in the name of Jesus, and then I prayed for all his muscles, ligaments, and tendons to be healed. Then the most extraordinary thing happened, the Holy Spirit fell on his wrist and his wrist was totally healed by Jesus. He took his brace off and bent his wrist backwards and forwards several times to show he was healed. Hallelujah! Kevin was not a Christian, but Jesus showed his love for him that day, and we gave him a gospel tract, said our goodbyes and went on our way. This, of course, is not a healing but a creative miracle as the Holy Spirit supernaturally healed his fractured wrist without any surgery whatsoever. If you pray for someone sick with a fever, it is called a healing, but if you pray for someone and Jesus gives them a new body part or heals a broken wrist, it is called a creative miracle.

Sometimes, the Holy Spirit can show up quite forcefully and people can be slain in the spirit. There is much controversy about this and it happened to me once when I was praying for a lady in a church in Harrogate in 2019. In this particular church, there was quite often a call at the end of the service for people to come forward for prayer, and that particular day I happened to be on the team. A lady came forward who said she was suffering from insomnia as her daughter had been in a car crash, had been very ill and she had spent years caring for her daughter. She had had interrupted nights for many years and was unable to sleep through the night anymore. The Holy Spirit told me to put my hand on her head and I started praying for all the insomnia to go in the name of Jesus. Absolutely nothing happened and then I received the word 'trauma' very clearly. This is why it is so important to listen to the Holy Spirit, who was telling me that the root of the problem was actually trauma, which was affecting her sleep. I then prayed for all the trauma to leave her. All of a sudden, she fell to the ground. I was unable to catch her as she fell sideways away from me. I want to say at this point that I absolutely did not push her over in any way. She was clearly very traumatised by all that had happened to her, and she was on the floor for a good five minutes as the Holy Spirit healed her from serious trauma. Five minutes later she got to her feet a different person, completely unhurt, happy and smiling. Sometimes people need very deep healing and I believe this phenomenon of being slain in the spirit happens to people who need deep emotional healing.

I have often wondered if Jesus heals our pets and I have also prayed for animals occasionally when my friends' pets are sick. I remember the very first time I prayed for a dog many years ago when my neighbour's dog had been kicked badly by a horse. It was touch and go whether she was going to go blind in her eye as she had been kicked very close to one of her eyes. The dog was in shock after the accident and had stopped barking completely. I prayed for healing for the eye and for the dog to be healed of all trauma, and sure enough, the dog's eye completely healed. She did not go blind, started barking again immediately, and returned to her normal perky self within thirty minutes.

Another time, a friend rang me when I was driving in the car down to London to tell me she was very worried about her cat Barney as he had a urine infection and was losing blood in his urine, which was not responding to the prescribed antibiotics. (I have a hands-free system for my phone in the car). Barney was also by now not drinking or eating at all and the vet was advising my friend to think about having the cat put down. I felt the Holy Spirit tell me that we needed to pray immediately for the cat whose life was in danger, so I started to pray, asking the Holy Spirit to come upon Barney immediately to heal his kidneys and heal the urine infection. Then I prayed for all the bleeding to stop and for the cat to get her appetite back again so that he would start eating and drinking again. I thought no more about it, to be honest, for the rest of the day as I had a busy day that day, but that night, I received a video from my friend saying his bleeding had stopped and showed Barney lapping up a huge bowl of milk. Barney is still very fit and well to this day, and I am absolutely sure that our prayers that day saved his life. I still have that video on my phone and love watching it! Jesus loves our animals just as much as we do, and he proved it that day by completely healing Barney after we prayed for him. Hallelujah!

My favourite healing though is of an elderly lady who is 82 and lives in Arkansas in the USA. She contacted me for prayer for healing on Zoom in December 2023 as she was suffering from severe pain and couldn't sleep. She had serious back problems and had undergone four back surgeries, and now, as a result of old age, arthritis had set in. She contacted me as she was suffering from severe pain in her back day and night and was completely unable to sleep at night, even after taking painkillers every four hours. I scheduled a Zoom call for her in December. When Henrietta came on the call, she told me she was still in immense pain and unable to sleep at night so I prayed hard for her, commanding all the pain to go in the name of Jesus. Next, I prayed for all the arthritis to go and for her spine to be restored. She sent me a text five minutes after the Zoom call: "This very minute, I don't have pain for the first time in 5-6 days. Amazed and awed. I can't thank you enough".

She contacted me again three months later with another text: "Since our healing session, I have not had a bad episode. It took a while, and I do still have issues with my back, but not the bad pain I was having. To God be the Glory".

I simply love this testimony as we rarely hear of the elderly being healed of arthritis, but God is sovereign, and he is able to do it. We just have to ask and he will answer our prayers even across Zoom to a different country on the other side of the world. God is omnipresent, omniscient and omnipotent. He sees everything, knows everything, and is still in control. He will heal us if we ask him to. As Henrietta says, "To God be the glory!".

Chapter Three

Words Of Knowledge

"To the listening ear I speak, to the waiting heart I come. Sometimes I may not speak. I may ask you merely to wait in my presence, to know that I am with you."[12]

Another tool that God uses to convey messages to people is the gift of knowledge, one of the gifts of the Holy Spirit. For those who are unchurched or have never come across it before, this gift is when people speak under the power of the Holy Spirit and are given divine knowledge that they couldn't possibly know. It is very similar to the gift of prophecy, but

---

[12] God Calling: A Devotional Diary

prophetic words usually pertain to the future, whereas a word of knowledge will describe something or someone in the present or in the past. The gift of prophecy and the gift of knowledge are clearly evident throughout the Old Testament and the New Testament.

For centuries, God raised up prophets in Israel, and the Kings of Israel relied on them to tell them whether he was with them in battle and whether they would be victorious over their enemies. Sometimes a prophet was sent by God to rebuke the King, as in the case of King David. We all know the story of the Prophet Nathan, who was sent to King David after he had committed adultery with Bathsheba and, even worse, had deliberately sent her husband Uriah to his death by sending him to the front line. God sent Nathan to King David, who told him a parable of a rich man taking a poor man's only ewe, thereby confronting King David with his adultery.[13] As a result of this word of knowledge, King David repented fully of his actions and wrote the beautiful Psalm 51 of repentance. He was reconciled back to God as a result of his sincere repentance, but he was punished for his

---

[13] 2 Samuel 12:1-4

disobedience. Bathsheba's child died, and his reign was plunged into civil war.

There are so many wonderful stories in the Old Testament of Elijah, a great prophet of God who announced a prophetic word given to him by the Lord that there would be no rain or dew in Israel for 3 years due to the sins of King Ahab who was eviler than all the previous rulers of Israel. He called fire down from heaven during his confrontation with the false prophets of Baal on the top of Mount Carmel, which towers over the plain of Armageddon.[14]

Miracles of provision happened as well. When the brook that he had been drinking from dried up, God sent him to Zarephath to a widow who fed him with her last remaining piece of bread. To repay her kindness, he declared over her now empty pot of flour and jar of oil that the jar of flour would not be used up and the jug of oil would not run dry until the day that rain came once more on the land of Israel. His prophetic word came true, and her oil and flour didn't run out until the famine ended years later.[15] He was perhaps the greatest Old Testament prophet from Israel and was rewarded for his obedience to God by

---

[14] 2 Kings 1:10
[15] 1 Kings 17:16

being taken to heaven in a whirlwind.

Time and time again through the ages, God sent prophets to Israel to tell her that he was with her in battle and would not forsake her, and there are many stories in the Old Testament that show God's protection over the nation of Israel during war. Aside from God parting the Red Sea[16] and destroying the entire Egyptian army in its wake, another famous story which portrays God's protection in battle over the nation of Israel is, of course, the story of David killing the giant Goliath with a single stone to his head.[17]

Another example is the story of the defeat of the Amalekites in the book of Exodus when Moses tells Joshua to choose some of their strongest men to go out and fight against the Amalekites who had attacked them. Moses went to the top of the hill with his staff to overlook the battle, and as long as Moses kept his arms up, the Israelites were winning, but if he lowered his arms, the Amalekites were winning. The battle raged all day, and, in the end, Aarib and Hur had to hold his hands up until sunset, and Joshua

---

[16] Exodus 14:21-22
[17] 1 Samuel 17:49

therefore defeated the Amalekites that day.[18]

On my holiday to Israel, I visited the site of the 7th Brigade tank monument and museum in the Golan Heights and learnt for myself of God's supernatural protection of the nation of Israel during the Yom Kippur War. On 6 October 1973 on Yom Kippur, which is the holiest day of the year for the Israeli people, the military base in the Golan Heights near the border with Syria was bombed. This was a deliberate surprise attack which caught the Israeli military by surprise as they would have been resting and fasting that day, Yom Kippur being a holy day of atonement for the Jews. When they got to the border, they found 800 brand-new Russian tanks advancing towards them. They only had 100 tanks, so they were outgunned by 8 to 1. After several days of very fierce fighting, the Israelis were down to two tanks in one division. The commanding officer therefore gave the command to retreat, but a very brave Brigadier General Kalahani chose deliberately to ignore that command as he knew that many civilians would lose their lives if they did. He ordered all the tanks closest to him to go to a hill behind him and to point the tanks

---

[18] Exodus 17:10

down at the Syrians. This gave them an advantage point, and they managed to achieve victory over the advancing Syrian tanks in 3 hours, who then subsequently retreated. We learnt that Brigadier General Kalahani was the Brigadier of the 7th Armoured Brigade of the 77th Battalion. If you are interested in numbers like me, this speaks volumes. 7 is the number for Jesus Christ, and Jesus was clearly guiding this very brave Brigadier on that fateful day and was behind him all the way. I asked my tour guide if the Israeli children were being taught about this incredible victory at school, to which I received the reply,

"No because we don't teach miracles at school!"

God will never forsake Israel, and the story above is a wonderful illustration of Jesus's protection in battle during the Yom Kippur War in 1973.

It is Jesus, King of Kings and Priests of Priests, as Melchizedek was both King and priest, who was the master of the prophetic, as you would expect, as he is the Son of God. There are many examples of this, but one of the most obvious is when he tells his disciples to prepare for the Last Supper and instructs them to find a man carrying a pitcher of water to follow him into the house and gives very precise instructions of what they are to say to the man to clinch a furnished room in which to host Jesus's last meal with his disciples. When his disciples get to the city, they do find a man with a bucket of water, and they follow him to the house. There is a room upstairs for them, and it is just as Jesus foretold in his prophetic word.[19]

Another clear example is when Jesus meets the Samaritan woman at the well. She had had five husbands and this lady was ostracised by the local women who obviously thought she was rather a loose woman. She therefore went to draw water from the well in the midday sun to avoid the local woman who would have all drawn water at the well first thing in the morning.[20] Jesus though, instead of judging her and mocking her, shows great kindness and mercy towards her. He tells her that he knows she has had five husbands as he is the Son of God and says to her that he is the Messiah they have all been waiting for, and he will supply her with living water, that is the Holy Spirit. He informs her that these living waters will nourish her and satisfy her if she is willing to give her life to him. The transformation in this lady after her encounter with Jesus is astonishing. In one

---

[19] Mark 14:13-15
[20] John 4:17-18

conversation and a word of knowledge from Jesus, she has a living encounter with the Messiah, her shame vanishes and she becomes an evangelist running off to her local town to tell them she has met the Messiah who told her everything she had ever done.

The Pharisees did their very best to test Jesus and to outsmart him, but they failed dismally every time as Jesus was full to overflowing with the gift of wisdom and the gift of knowledge. The gift of wisdom is very similar to the gift of knowledge. You could say the gift of knowledge is knowing what to say, but the gift of wisdom is knowing when to say it. They asked him whether it was right to give the imperial tax to Caesar, and he knew that they were trying to trip him up. He gave a brilliant reply, telling them that they should give to Caesar what is Caesar's and to God what is God's.[21]

The Sadducees then tried to trip Jesus up when they tested him with the story of a woman who had been married to 7 brothers, and asked Jesus whose wife she was. Again, he gave them a brilliant reply and said that there is no marriage in heaven as everyone

---

[21] Matthew 22:21

is holy like the angels; in other words, their question is irrelevant. Jesus then continues saying that in any case God is the God of Abraham, Isaac and Jacob, the God of the living and not of the dead.[22] Jesus decides to then put the Pharisees to the test and asked them who they think is the Son of God. They reply that they think he is the son of David. Jesus filled with the gift of knowledge and the gift of wisdom, gives the most brilliant reply, saying how can he be the Son of King David if King David calls him Lord and quotes Psalm 110 to illustrate his point.[23] This silences the Pharisees completely and they stopped questioning him anymore after that, as Jesus had the gift of knowledge and the gift of wisdom, and he had it in spades. It is important to realise that Jesus always spoke what the Holy Spirit and God the Father told him to say and it was always truthful, as Jesus is the embodiment of grace and truth.[24]

Sadly, the gift of knowledge and the gift of prophecy are not commonplace in many traditional churches nowadays and I say this to our detriment. I will be forever grateful to the three people who had

---

[22] Matthew 22:29-32
[23] Psalm 110:1
[24] 1 John 5:6

the courage to walk up to me and give me a word of knowledge from the Lord that he wanted me to write, as it encouraged me to do so, and I probably would never have embarked on writing anything if they hadn't been obedient to the Lord and delivered the word to me.

Words of knowledge should be uplifting and encouraging. I will never forget a word of knowledge given to me at a Christian conference in Cwmbran in 2022, where we were all encouraged to pair up with someone we didn't know. I waved to a blonde lady at the other side of the room who I had said hello to that morning for the first time and she came over to me as she was not supposed to team up with her husband. What I hadn't realised was that this lady was extremely prophetic. She told me that God had given her a picture of me with a bow and arrow and that he was preparing me for battle. She also told me that Jesus wanted me to dance as I had done as a young girl. That word really blessed me and was an entirely accurate description of my life at the time. I was not fighting in the physical realm but God was definitely using me to fight in the spiritual realm and her word was a confirmation of this. This lady wasn't speaking at the conference, she had simply come to the conference like me but God had blessed her with the gift of knowledge, and she was not afraid to speak it out. Hallelujah!!

I had an experience just before Christmas when I went to a drinks party, and God put me to the test to see if I would be obedient and speak out the words he gave me for someone I had never met before. I was introduced to a man who said he was an international aid worker. I assumed he would be a Christian and asked him whether he was one as I was interested to hear his reply. He then told me that he was not a Christian because he had spent his life for the last 20 years flying to war zones, feeding those displaced by war and setting up first aid facilities. This had clearly been very demanding work and he told me that he had seen so much trauma caused by war that he had no faith. He then proceeded to tell us all the countries and war zones that he had been to. This gave me a few minutes to pray and ask Jesus what he wanted me to say to this man. I silently prayed, asking for a word of knowledge to bring him to the Lord. The Holy Spirit told me very clearly what to say. So, I said to him,

"Don't you realise that you have been an absolute lifeline providing food and emergency medical care to thousands of people all over the world for twenty years and that you have, in actual fact, been doing God's work all this time?"

I carried on. The Holy Spirit also showed me that he had been protecting this man the entire time, so I also said to him,

"Not only that, but don't you realise that God has been protecting you all this time. It is an absolute miracle that you haven't been shot or blown up when you have been working in so many conflicts."

I told him that he had clearly led the most fascinating life that people would love to hear about and that he ought to write it all down in a memoir. He was silent for a minute whilst he processed all that I said to him, and I knew the Holy Spirit was at work because he suddenly said to me and the lady who was with me,

"Gosh, you are right. I hadn't thought of it like that. Yes, it is a miracle that I have not been shot or badly injured. Let's all link arms, and I am going to lead you all in a prayer."

So, all three of us joined arms whilst this dear man led us in prayer in the middle of a drinks party! That's when you really know that someone has been touched by the Holy Spirit and I thank God that Jesus told me what to say and gave me the key to unlock his heart and bring him to Christ. Sometimes the words we speak can be very powerful, especially if they come from the Holy Spirit. The Holy Spirit is the spirit of prophecy, and it always bears testimony to Jesus Christ because the Holy Spirit is truth. How we need the gift of knowledge and the gift of prophecy, and may it flow in ALL our churches once more!

Chapter Four

Deliverance

Darkness cannot drive out darkness; only light can do that. Hate cannot drive out hate; only love can do that.[25]

This is another very important topic, and I believe many people in our society today need deliverance as there is so much filth nowadays everywhere we look from our television screens, which are filled with sexual content, the cinema, not to mention sordid magazines and newspapers. It is all around us. Many too are seduced by the lie that yoga and the new age are totally safe and harmless. They are not. Yoga

_____

[25] Martin Luther King Jr - Good Reads Online

poses are in actual fact Hindu poses, and therefore, in God's eyes, yoga is worshipping other Gods and if you do yoga frequently, it can let in an evil spirit called the Kundalini Spirit. The Kundalini spirit is a serpent-like Spirit and is a manifestation of the spirit of divination, which we read about in Acts 16:16. In Sanskrit, the word 'kund' means to burn and 'kunda' is to coil or to spiral. In Hinduism, it is commonly accepted that a spiritual snake is coiled up in each person's back. A direct translation of the word 'kundalini' is 'serpent power', which is why some translations call this spirit of divination the 'snake-spirit' or a spirit of Python. Many people think yoga is totally harmless, but once the Kundalini spirit comes in, it can cause depression, mental illness and demonic oppression.

The New Age and meditation are also very attractive to the young but they are equally dangerous and can cause evil spirits to come in as they are a form of idolatry. At schools, they are teaching children to meditate and to practise mindfulness, but Jesus NEVER ever taught his disciples to meditate. He taught them to pray and told them that he is the way, the truth and the life, that there is no other route to heaven, except by repenting of our sins and accepting Jesus as our Lord and Saviour. Meditation will not bring you peace as in Jesus's eyes, he sees it as worshipping other Gods, and therefore, if you meditate you are committing paganism.

Last summer I prayed for a lady in a conference in Scotland who was born into an Indian family but is now a Christian. She had practiced yoga and meditation often growing up, and she told me she had been ill for years and remembered that when she was young, she had drunk some tea in a Hindu temple. She told me that also at night she slept very badly and dreamt of evil spirits. I told her she needed deliverance and we took her to a back room at the conference and started praying for her. Immediately she started coughing very frequently, and my colleague who was helping me said she could see a snake coiled around her neck. Immediately I prayed Psalm 91 over her, in particular the verse which talks about treading on and trampling on the serpent. She shrieked and the power of God fell on her and she was completely set free of the Kundalini spirit which had been affecting her for years. Hallelujah!

I have also encountered the Kundalini spirit on Zoom when I was serving on the ministry team of an international ministry that I was a member of for four years. A lady who I will call Tessa came on in August 2022 who was brought up as a Christian but had started doing yoga and classes with a Hindu guru.

Ever since then, she had been sick, was in great pain and was suffering from kidney failure and liver damage. She also had swollen ankles. I asked her to repent of the yoga classes and of going to see the guru which she did immediately. I then recognised that this was the Kundalini Spirit and started praying in tongues over her, casting the evil spirit out in the name of Jesus. One minute later, the Holy Spirit showed up in force and hit her like a truck, and she started coughing for about five minutes, as the Holy Spirit literally drove all the sickness out of her. I also prayed in tongues over her at the end, asking the Holy Spirit to fill her so that no more evil spirits would get back in.

Two months later, she returned to the meeting and testified in public that she had gone to the doctor again, that her kidneys and liver were now completely normal, that all the pain in her body was gone, and that her ankles were now completely normal. What a wonderful God we have!! She was completely delivered from this evil spirit and completely healed as well because when an evil spirit is cast out, there is always subsequent healing. It is very important to give all the glory to Jesus for her healing and not take any credit for it ourselves. We pray, but it is always the Holy Spirit that heals and delivers people from evil spirits.

I hope these testimonies are giving you a clear picture of how dangerous the New Age and yoga is. The devil always comes as an angel of light, but it is only Jesus who is the real light who overcomes all darkness, and he is the only way we can reach heaven when we die. There is no other route. He carries eternal life because he paid the price on the cross for us to be forgiven of all our sins.

Pornography is another portal that allows demons to enter the human body. Sadly, this has increased dramatically with the rise of the internet, and I know that it is a real problem in today's world. It has also caused sexual sin to proliferate, which is now widely accepted. So many couples choose to live together outside of marriage nowadays and the word 'partner' is commonplace, but the word of God doesn't change; it doesn't bend to societal norms. Living with someone outside of marriage is displeasing in the eyes of God. There is a remedy and it is called MARRIAGE. Jesus desires us to lead holy lives as our bodies are temples of the Holy Spirit and marriage is a sacrament, and therefore holy in the eyes of God. If you have committed any sexual sin, it is extremely important to repent. I have prayed for several people who have admitted that they have been looking at pornography and all of them repented and were subsequently healed and restored by the power of God. What a loving and merciful God we have! The following testimony is of a man we prayed for in the summer of 2023 who was completely healed and restored from severe depression, which had got in from looking at pornography when he was a young man.

Last summer, I was asked to go on an emergency visit to a gentleman who was suffering from severe depression and was even having suicidal thoughts. Laura and I decided that this was too serious to be dealt with in a Filling Station meeting, so we asked him if we could come to him instead. We were going south to near his neck of the woods so we decided that we would drop by his house and pray for him at home. I remember it was the most glorious sunny day last April 2023. He lives in the most glorious spot right out in the countryside with hills and sheep all around him. The Holy Spirit told me straight away that he needed deliverance of an evil spirit. He is happily married, but the evil spirit was very much tormenting him and making him very depressed.

When we arrived, the gentleman told us that he thought this depression had come in as a result of looking at pornographic magazines when he was a young man before he was married. So, we asked him to repent of looking at pornography and to repent of anything else that he might have committed as a young man, for example, fornication. After he had finished repenting, we led him through the sinner's prayer. Then, we started praying in tongues over him, asking the Holy Spirit to come into the room and set this dear man free. Suddenly he completely changed, was unable to sit upright anymore and he started to manifest a very large demon. He was unable to control his hands; they curled up into a ball-like shape, and he started making rather ugly, demonic noises through his mouth, growling at us. I then immediately realised that this was no small demon, and I addressed it by saying,

"Spirit of pornography, come out of him now in the name of Jesus!"

Immediately, the demon started speaking to us and said,

"I am Asmodeus, and I am not coming out!"

Laura and I didn't know who Asmodeus is. I recognised that it was a Latin name but didn't know what it was. Laura quickly went onto her phone and looked up Asmodeus; we discovered that he is extremely dangerous and one of the seven princes of hell. Asmodeus is the demon of LUST, which can come in through pornography, fornication and adultery.

Once we knew that Asmodeus was the demon of lust, we knew that the battle was won. So, both Laura and I shouted,

"Demon of lust, your time is up. Get out of him now in the name of Jesus!"

The man then started saying over and over again, "I am weak! I am weak!" He then gave a very loud shriek after the evil spirit left him, and there was much rejoicing in the room, as you can imagine. We let him rest for five minutes, as deliverance can be very tiring, and then we prayed once again, asking the Holy Spirit to fill him back up. This is very important. Jesus commanded his disciples to always do this, in order that seven more demons do not come back in in the future. We were all over the moon, and we have heard from the gentleman in question since that day, and he is now in flying form with no depression and much happier. We left a very happy man that day, and Laura and I left rejoicing all the way back home.

Addiction to cigarettes, alcohol abuse and drug abuse are also, of course, very dangerous as they cause spirits of addiction to come in, which in turn can lead to depression and wreak havoc on a person's health. I have had personal experience of this as my mother was an alcoholic when I was a young child, and she had to go into a rehab clinic. Fortunately, she was healed and never drank again for the rest of her life.

Jesus however can heal people of addiction and very successfully. I prayed for a lady in a Filling Station meeting who was on forty cigarettes a day and now she is not smoking at all. All glory to Jesus! We haven't had any alcoholics coming to our meetings, but Jesus absolutely can and does heal people who are addicted to alcohol and drugs. Jackie Pullinger has written a book about her ministry to help drug addicts in Hong Kong and has spent her life getting drug addicts off the streets and healing them by bringing them to faith and praying in tongues over them. None of them go to rehab clinics. They are all healed by the power of God.

This is the testimony of a young man called Tony who was a heroin addict but repented of his sins and accepted Jesus as his Saviour. He was healed of drug addiction through the power of tongues,

"They prayed for me and I accepted Jesus as my Lord and I received the baptism of the Spirit. At first,

I felt very cold but when I was filled with the Spirit a very surprising thing happened – I felt my heart burning within me and my whole body grew warm and I wept. I had not cried since I was a child. I sat shamelessly weeping in front of everyone, and I knew that I had become 'born again'.

They took me to Stephen's Third House to come off heroin. I had tried many times to come off drugs. The pain had always been greater than I could bear. The first time I went to prison, I had to come off 'cold turkey', and it was so terrible that I broke out of prison into barbed wire and still bear the scars to this day. From that day, I always had heroin hidden on my person so that I was never caught without it. But this time it was different. My brother in Jesus prayed for me and I also prayed in tongues and the pain disappeared. Two months later I went to live with Mr and Mrs Williams who run the houses."[26]

The last topic I want to mention is the question of generational curses, as these can come in if a member of your family, a parent or a grandparent has been involved in witchcraft or freemasonry. According to the book of Exodus, these can curse families for three

---

[26] Chasing the Dragon p.161 by Jackie Pullinger

or four generations and cause sickness in children or grandchildren. The context of this scripture is actually talking about the sin of worshipping other Gods and idolatry, but it is also relevant to freemasonry and witchcraft.

I was in a Zoom meeting in 2022 when a middle-aged lady came on who had come from a family in which her father had been involved in witchcraft and the occult. She no longer saw her father as a grown up, but she told us that he was still sending her letters, and she was concerned that he was putting spells or curses on the letters and was very worried about this.

I began praying in tongues over her and started to bind the spirit of witchcraft and asking the Holy Spirit to cast it out of her in the name of Jesus. Immediately, the Holy Spirit fell on her, and she bent over and started coughing it all out for about five minutes. Then we let her rest for a minute or two before praying in tongues over her again, asking the Holy Spirit to fill her back up. She left happy, smiling and full of peace, which was a joy to see. We also told her to destroy all the letters that her father had sent her, as curses can be transferred onto letters and other objects if they have been sent by someone involved in the occult and witchcraft.

The extraordinary thing was that in the same meeting, a young man came on and he also was concerned about the spirit of witchcraft as he also had family members who were involved in the occult. We led him in a prayer of repentance and said the salvation prayer with him. Again, we started praying in tongues over him, and he started coughing for five minutes. We broke all generational curses off him in the name of Jesus and he left at peace, very happy, smiling and praising God. Finally, we prayed in tongues over both of them to be filled up and for them both to receive the gift of the tongues. What a wonderful God we serve that by the end of the call, both of them were set free from the spirit of witchcraft and generational curses. Glorious Day!

If I am praying for someone whose family member has been involved with or is currently involved with the occult, I always lead them through a prayer of repentance on behalf of their family member to break off any generational curses as such curses can last for three or four generations. If a family member is involved in witchcraft or in freemasonry too, it can negatively affect their children and their grandchildren, so it is very important that these generational curses are broken off.[27]

I was on a Zoom call recently with a lady whose husband had passed away. When he was alive, he had become mentally ill and he had gone home to his native country to see his mother. His mother persuaded him to go to a voodoo witch doctor, and this affected the entire family as they had become seriously ill. We therefore prayed for all curses to be broken off the family and led his wife through a prayer of repentance. She returned to us a week later, saying there was a definite improvement in her spirits and health. Hallelujah!

It is also important to note that sometimes people can have more than one evil spirit inside them. I remember praying for one man in a meeting, and the Holy Spirit showed him that he had a nest of snakes inside him, which let me know that there were several evil spirits that needed to come out. When that happens, and there are multiple spirits involved, that is when you need the gift of discernment of spirits to discern who the 'strong man' is. Once you know that and cast the 'strong man' out, the rest will come out easily. I have prayed for several people who have

---

27 Exodus 20:5-6

picked up the spirit of Jezebel from dabbling in the occult or witchcraft, as demonstrated above. She is one of the spirits strongly associated with witchcraft and the occult. She is very high up in the demonic realm but she is however no match for the power of the Holy Spirit when you quote the word of God at her, as demonstrated by the testimonies above.

Finally, on my trip to Israel I visited a place called Banyas in the North. It used to be a very demonic place two thousand years ago as the Pan God, half man and half goat, was worshipped at a temple there consecrated to Pan and Zeus. The very beautiful river Dan flows there, which actually runs down further south into the river Jordan. They used to sacrifice goats in the river and commit all sorts of immorality as they literally believed the place was a gateway to hell. The remains of a temple are still there to this day but Jesus took his disciples there as a teaching point to teach them that they would have power over evil, to cast out demons because the Holy Spirit in us is greater than the power of evil in the world. This teaching still applies to all of us who are whole-heartedly seeking Jesus and who are interested in deliverance; we have the power to trample on snakes and scorpions TODAY and set people free in the name of Jesus. Fasting is key for those who are interested in praying for deliverance for others, as it gives glory to God and strengthens us spiritually, as this battle is not physical, against flesh and blood but spiritual.

Chapter Five

Angels

We may be very ordinary, but God wants to make us extraordinary in the Holy Spirit.

In various religious traditions such as Judaism and Christianity, an angel is a supernatural spiritual being who serves God. The word angel derives from the Old English 'engel' and the Old French 'angele'. Both of these derive from the Latin 'angelus', which in turn was borrowed from the Greek 'angelos', which means "messenger". In the Protestant churches, the Anglican tradition recognises three Archangels, Michael the warrior Archangel, and Gabriel the Archangel who we all know was sent to announce to Mary that she was going to conceive and give birth to a son, Jesus. There is also Raphael the Archangel of healing, mentioned in the book of Tobit, which falls in the Apocrypha section of the Roman Catholic bible. (Archangel Uriel is another Archangel, which means "fire of God", and Archangel Jeramneel, which means "God's mercy." They are mentioned in the book of Esdras, which is also in the Apocrypha section of the Roman Catholic bible. Uriel and Jeramneel are not widely known in the Protestant church as they are mentioned in the Apocrypha, but they are recognised in the Anglican Communion). Archangels are chief angels; the English word archangel is derived from the Greek arkhangelos, the Greek prefix "arch" meaning chief.

Michael in the Hebrew language means "Who is like God?" He has been depicted from earliest times as a soldier who holds a spear with which he attacks the devil in his right hand, and in his left hand, he holds a green palm branch. At the top of the spear, there is a linen ribbon with a red cross. He is considered to be the Guardian of the Faith and fights against heresy. Gabriel in Hebrew means "God is my strength". He is the messenger of the incarnation of God and he is the herald of the will of God. He is depicted holding a lantern with a lighted lantern in his right hand and a mirror of green jasper in his left hand. The mirror signifies the wisdom of God. (I was very interested to find out recently that in one of the main squares of Kiev in Ukraine, there is a huge statue of Archangel Michael and there have been sightings of a huge archangel in the skies over Kiev during the war with Russia. Archangel Michael is the warrior Archangel, so it has to be him.) Raphael is a Hebrew name which means 'God heals'. Raphael is depicted with a spear in his right hand, holding a physician's alabaster jar in his left hand as he is the Archangel of healing.

A common misconception is that archangels are the highest rank of angels in Christianity, whereas in fact, they are the second lowest rank of angel in the Christian hierarchy of angels put forward by Pseudo-Dionysius the Areopagite in the 5th or 6th century in his book De Doelesti Hierarchia. There are nine ranks of angels; thrones, dominions, principalities, seraphim, cherubim, powers, sovereignties, archangels and angels. There are also guardian angels who are lower than archangels, and every single person on earth has a guardian angel assigned to them during their time on earth to protect them.

In the bible the existence of angels, just like that of demons is taken for granted. They dwell in the heavens and worship God but they also protect us in times of danger. It is so significant that a multitude of angels proclaim the birth of Jesus in the adoration of the shepherds, but I also love Mary's encounter with an angel after the death of Jesus which is so moving. Just after the resurrection of Jesus an angel appears to Mary and another woman also called Mary when they go to visit Jesus's tomb after his crucifixion. An angel rolls away the stone and is sitting on it. He is described as having a countenance like lightening and his clothing is as white as snow. The guards are described as fainting from fear when they see this majestic angel from heaven. The angel consoles the women and tells them to not be afraid, that Jesus is not there because he is risen from the dead. He then invites them to go inside the tomb to check for themselves and instructs them to go and tell the disciples that Jesus is risen from the dead and that he has gone to Galilee, where they can find him. What a glorious encounter![28]

There are also many angelic encounters in the Old Testament. Two angels accompany Jesus to tell Abraham that his wife Sara is going to give birth in

---

[28] Matthew 28:1-7

her old age. An angel appeared in front of Balaam and his donkey, blocking his route and terrifying the donkey, another angel appeared to Elijah and brought him breakfast in the wilderness when he was starving and on the run from King Ahab and Queen Jezebel. I find it completely astonishing that Archangel Gabriel appeared to the prophet Daniel to explain his visions and gave him a prophesy which directly relates to the end times we are living in thousands of years later. Gabriel prophesied war in Israel, which is happening now, and foretold that a purported 'man of peace' will rise up to negotiate a peace treaty for one week (seven years) with `many' to end the war in Israel.[29]

In a later vision, Daniel is shown another end-times event, that Archangel Michael will rise up to protect the people in the end times and that there will be a time of trouble, but that during that time, all those who are found written in the book of life will be delivered.[30] That sounds to me distinctly like the rapture of the church when Jesus sends his angels out to rescue believing Christians, both alive and deceased. It is written in the book of Daniel that many also who sleep, that is have died will AWAKE,

---

[29] Daniel 9:27
[30] Daniel 12:1

referring to the resurrection of the dead, which Jesus foretold, that all those who die in Christ will be taken to heaven in the resurrection of the dead at the rapture.

I am deeply saddened by the terrible war in Gaza to hear how many innocent people have died on both sides but also very alarmed to see the rise of antisemitism, which seems to be rearing its ugly head once more; what they are not covering is the GOOD news of the miracles that are happening in Gaza. There are many stories of the miraculous happening to the Israeli army in Gaza, showing that God is helping them and saving them from danger every step of the way. I went to a talk last night given by Christian Friends of Israel, and she told several miraculous stories that have been narrated to them by soldiers in the IDF.

One story that happened recently is of an IDF commander who was on patrol with his regiment in Gaza, and he was suffering from sleep deprivation as he had had no sleep for 36 hours as they were on duty. They had been sent on a life and death mission to a certain block in Gaza to find a huge stache of explosives that had been hidden in a building in Gaza. Suddenly a white dove flew in front of the commander and his regiment and started flapping its wings directly in front of the officer. The soldier behind him pulled the commanding officer back, and the dove remained flapping its wings. They looked to where the dove was and saw a trip wire. If the commanding officer had taken another step forward, he would have walked into the trip wire and the entire area would have been blown up, including the commanding officer and his entire regiment. Jesus obviously sent a dove to save the commanding officer's life and his regiment, which is amazing because all the birds and animals had left that part of Gaza.

Another soldier has told how he was saved from being killed by a sniper's bullet by a book of Psalms, which he put in his shirt pocket that day. Normally he did not put a book in his shirt pocket but that particular day he decided to put a book of psalms in his pocket. He was shot in the chest that day but the book took the bullet and saved him from being killed.

The most amazing story of them all is the story of a mysterious rabbi appearing to a regiment in Gaza whose job was to find the Hamas tunnels in Gaza. They had found a tunnel in a building and usually the commanding officer goes first down the tunnel with five or six soldiers while the rest of the regiment stay outside and surround the house. The radio guy tried to ring his commanding officer and there was no answer. They went into the house and found the tunnel and they saw a rabbi at the entrance to the tunnel with a long beard and wearing a hat. They said to him,

"What are you doing in this house?"

The rabbi replied and said to them,

"You must get out of the house now! If you don't get out of the house now, there will be many widows and orphans. You have to leave now!"

The sergeant replied that they couldn't leave, as they had to go into the tunnel to find out where his commanding officer was. The Rabbi replied again that they had to leave immediately. He then tried to push the Rabbi out of the way and his hand went right through the Rabbi. The soldiers by now are in total shock as they realise, they are not talking to a human Rabbi! The commanding officer then came out of the tunnel and tried to push the Rabbi out of the way, and he and six more soldiers walked right through him. The Rabbi then talked to them all again and said,

"I am begging you; you must leave the house NOW!!!"

At this point fire was coming out of the Rabbis mouth and all the soldiers were now freaking out. The soldiers then all ran out of the house, and when they got 20 steps outside of the house, it blew sky high. The appearance of the unknown Rabbi is known as a Christophany, an appearance of Christ after his resurrection in disguise. As you can imagine these stories are having an amazing effect on all the soldiers in the army and are bringing them to faith very fast! They are realising that there is a God who is protecting them and saving their lives. There are many more stories like these which are coming out of Israel.

Jesus also is trying desperately to reach the innocent Palestinian civilians who have been caught up in the war in Gaza as he wants to save everyone, and that includes the Palestinian civilians who live in Gaza. Many Palestinian men, women and children are being cared for by Christian aid organisations working in Gaza. Many of them have lost family members because of the war and therefore are suffering deep emotional pain. It was recently reported that an angel appeared to a group of twenty Palestinian women with their children in Gaza who were trapped in a hideout and had run out of food and water due to the war. A man suddenly appeared at the door, wearing a white robe and led them to a safe place away from the bombing where there was food and water. Once they arrived at the house, he departed, giving them a note with the words John 3:16 on it. The women discovered John 3:16 is a Christian verse, were absolutely amazed and realised that it was an angel who had appeared to them and led them to safety. Did those women see an angel or an archangel? Who knows, but it was definitely a heavenly being sent to help them in their hour of need. Jesus and his angels are on the move amidst all the suffering in Gaza, not just saving the lives of the IDF soldiers but also appearing to many civilian Palestinian men and women. The scripture from the book of Joel seems to be coming to pass right now, not just in Gaza but worldwide, old men are dreaming dreams and young men and women are seeing visions as the Holy Spirit is being poured out.[31]

The gift of seeing angels is called seeing in the spirit, either in visions, dreams, "knowing" or actually seeing with our natural eyes. I know a lady who received this gift quite late on in life, as a grown-up, which is unusual because as children, we have this ability, but when we grow up, most of us lose this gift. This is her testimony,

"At first, all I saw with my eyes were streaks and

---

[31] Joel 2:28-29

flashes of colour that coalesced into balls of swiftly moving swirling light. Over a matter of months, under the tutelage of the Holy Spirit, the orbs began to take the shape of fuzzy outlines resembling moving figures. Within a few weeks, I began to recognise the figures as people and the Holy Spirit explained to me that these were indeed angels engaged in their heaven-sent tasks, moving and working in and around my friends, family and coworkers. Eventually, I was blessed with seeing angels everywhere, from moving across the sky to the train station and began to understand with Holy Spirit's instruction, some of their roles and activities in our lives.

From my observations and experience, we appear to all have at least one personal angel who is with us at all times and never ever leaves our side. The angels look just like us – all shapes, sizes, hair colour and races. Although often robed, they sometimes wear trainers, whilst every now and then they are accompanied by fire, others just carry books or fruit, but all have one thing in common... they are infinitely more beautiful than any person I have ever seen. They appear to me ethereal, but reasonably solid, although sometimes I can see right through them. They often float, but usually walk, occasionally run and sometimes fly, even though they don't have wings. I now know that there are many types of angels, usually connected with the job they have been given – wisdom angel, protection angel, comfort, assistance and warrior etc. I see them pretty much everywhere I go now, although I am often bemused by the fact that I still don't expect to see them, and the Lord often surprises me by showing me something new and delightful that I haven't seen before in regard to His very busy divine messengers.

One of the places I often see the most angels in one place at one time is in worship services. Sometimes there is so much to see there, I hardly know where to look first. As well as the angels which come in with the worshippers, there are angels who decorate the ceiling with ribbons, streamers and flags, angels in the aisles carrying golden bowls, large impressive-looking angels usually standing by the door and younger angels skipping round the children whilst they play. Whilst one of the more regular scenes I encounter is the angels that appear above and around those leading the worship, playing instruments or singing, their activity is never quite the same in every service. I have seen the angels adorn the worship band members with garlands and headdresses of flowers, shower them with rose petals from above, and even build a bower of roses and vines, complete with grapes, around them as they sing the Lord's praises to Him."

I do not have the gift of seeing in the spirit but I remember vividly when I was ten years old, I saw an angel kneeling and praying by the bedside of the little girl sleeping in the bunk bed next to me at boarding school. Many children I think are able to see in the spiritual realm but of course the older they get they lose that ability. I remember very clearly one night the year that my sister died. For some reason I did not want to join in with all the chatting after lights out in my dormitory. I was in the bottom bunk bed next to the window and the moonlight was streaming in through the window as the curtains were rather inadequate. For once I didn't feel like chatting with everyone as I was feeling tired that night. There was a child in the next-door bed to me, and for some reason, I decided to turn round and look at her. All of a sudden, I saw an iridescent white figure with a shawl over her head, kneeling and praying by her bedside. I knew instantly I was seeing a being from another realm and I became absolutely terrified and started screaming for several minutes. It wasn't a ghost as it was praying and looked very peaceful. The figure was there for five minutes and then floated up out of the window. Everyone asked me what the matter was and

I explained what I had seen but mysteriously I was the only person who had seen the angel in the room that night. It was not long after my sister had died and I had been feeling totally grief-stricken. Looking back now, I should not have been so frightened as it was obviously a heavenly being. I believe I saw the child's guardian angel. That vision was a real blessing for me because it showed me that Jesus loved me and that he was real, although I remember being very scared at the time. I believe Jesus was trying to comfort me after my sister's death, and he was showing me that although I felt alone, I wasn't as he was upholding me. Life can be very tough at times, especially when we lose loved ones. During those times we must remember the promises of Jesus, that he never leaves us or forsakes us.

Chapter Six

Baptism Of The Holy Spirit

If you will become childlike enough, if you will yield to God and let the Spirit have His say, God will fill you with the Holy Spirit[32]

I grew up in the Church of England. I was baptised as a baby, confirmed at 16 and very much thought of myself as a Christian. I followed the traditions of men like many others and I thought that it was enough to go to church on Sundays and sit quietly in the back of the church listening to the sermon each Sunday. And I probably would have spent the rest of my life like that if it had not been for my divorce when God

---

[32] Smith Wigglesworth Devotional p.397

literally intervened in my life in a very unexpected manner. I was suffering from acute depression at the time and was crying out to Jesus one night for help to come off the antidepressants I was on. That same night, I was given the sinner's prayer to say by the Holy Spirit and was literally told what to say when I didn't have a copy of it in the house. These were the words that I recited, "Lord Jesus, I repent of all my sins. Please forgive me. Please cleanse me of all sin with your precious blood. I believe that you died on the cross and rose again on the 3rd day. Lord Jesus, please come into my heart and fill me up with your Holy Spirit. Amen".

This prayer is all important because we are saved by grace and not by works and yet we are not encouraged to say it in traditional churches. It doesn't matter how often you go to church or the number of good works you do if you have never repented and verbally confessed Jesus as your Lord and Saviour. We all have to repent of our sins whilst we are alive on earth and accept what Jesus did for us on the cross, if we want our sins to be forgiven. When we repent of our sins and accept Jesus, the blood of Jesus pays the price for our sins to be cancelled out and forgiven because Jesus paid the price by dying on the cross for the salvation of mankind. I said this prayer in private in the privacy of my bedroom but it is more commonly used in church settings. What is important to the Lord is actually that you mean it with all your heart wherever you say it. I then went to sleep and received a dream from the Holy Spirit, which was a dream about being baptised in a river. It was as if Jesus was leading me by the hand and instructing me in the way I should go. The meaning of the dream was clear, that I should go and be baptised in water. Although I had been a Christian since my confirmation, I was now a born-again Christian. I felt an immediate difference in my spirits, and a great sense of peace washed over me. Smith Wigglesworth hits the nail on the head when he writes, "On the other hand, there is so much that a man receives when he is born again. He receives the first love and has a revelation of Jesus."[33]

This is what Jesus meant when he was talking to Nicodemus and said we must be 'born again.' The salvation prayer above is a fulfilment of the scripture in the book of Romans, which says if we repent of our sins and verbally confess Jesus as our Lord and Saviour, we will be saved. Jesus then goes on to say to Nicodemus you must be baptised in water and of the

---

[33] Smith Wigglesworth Devotional p.369

spirit to enter heaven, but it has to be done in the right order, baptism of water ideally first and then the baptism of the Holy Spirit. The baptism of water is extremely important as it is not just a physical cleansing but a spiritual cleansing as well. All my depression lifted after my water baptism and I felt a great joy come into my heart for the first time in a long time. You become a new creation in Christ, the old you is gone. The Holy Spirit is HOLY and we have to be cleaned up before the Holy Spirit can fill us. We are all born with the Holy Spirit inside us but in order to receive the gift of tongues, which is the evidence of the baptism of the Holy Spirit, we have to be a clean vessel, that is to have repented and ideally be baptised in water.

Jesus affirms the importance of both water baptism and the baptism of the Holy Spirit in the bible as he asks John to baptise him in the river Jordan, and when he arises out of the water, he receives the baptism of the Holy Spirit, which is symbolised by a dove.[34] John visibly sees the Holy Spirit coming upon Jesus after his water baptism. However, it is not until Pentecost that the Holy Spirit

---

34 Matthew 3:16

is poured out dramatically upon all twelve disciples when they are praying in an upper room and tongues of fire appear over all of them, meaning that they have been baptised in the Holy Spirit. Jesus appeared to them before Ascension Day informing them that they would all be receiving this gift in order to give them courage and power to be able to preach the gospel and pray for others.[35]

Smith Wigglesworth wrote very eloquently on the importance of the baptism of the Holy Spirit, "Oh, it always seems to me that the Gospel is robbed of its divine glory when we overlook this marvellous truth of the baptism of the Holy Spirit.... But whereas we have the well of salvation bubbling up inside us, we need to go on to a place where from within us will flow 'rivers of living water'."[36]

The 'rivers of living water' that Smith is referencing is the gift of tongues, which is the evidence that the baptism of the Holy Spirit gives the church DUNAMIS (Greek word for power) to fulfil the Great Commission to heal the sick, cast out demons, and to preach the gospel. That is why those of us who want to see God move in power must have the

---

[35] Luke 24:49
[36] Smith Wigglesworth Devotional p.381

baptism of the Holy Spirit. We are powerless without it. If we choose to live a life of righteousness and holiness, then God will bless us, and we will see signs and wonders once more, and he will use us for his glory. We will then become a vessel for honour, sanctified and able to be used by God for healing the sick, casting out demons and so on.[37] Moreover, the baptism of the Holy Spirit is available to all of us, not just a select few. Everyone, male and female, rich and poor, black and white, Jew and gentile, can receive it TODAY; we just have to ask for it. There is no partiality. Jesus died for the salvation of the whole world, but he also had to die so that the Holy Spirit could be poured out on ALL FLESH.[38] In the same way that a grain of wheat can't produce a crop unless it falls to the ground and dies first, Jesus had to die so that the Holy Spirit could be poured out on the disciples at Pentecost, and thereafter to Jews and Gentiles.

This is the meaning of the vision that was given to Peter when he dreamed of many different animals together in a sheet descending from above. He received the word that he couldn't call anything

---

[37] 2 Timothy 2:21
[38] John 12:24

unclean that God had pronounced fit to eat. The Jews, of course, follow a kosher diet and are forbidden to eat pork, but Jesus was instructing him to take the gospel to the Gentiles here as well as the Jews. As a result of this dream, he went to a Roman Centurion's house called Cornelius, who was seeking God and baptised him and his whole family in a town called Caesarea.[39] Peter was obedient to the vision he received, and for many, this story marks the birth of the gentile church. I visited Caesarea a year ago. It is an amazing place, full of Roman remains and there still remains a column there that says Pilate was the prefect there two thousand years ago, which is clear archaeological proof that Pilate was indeed the Roman prefect responsible for sentencing Jesus to death.

The Holy Spirit is still baptising people today, and I have seen several people baptised in front of my eyes with the Holy Spirit on and off Zoom. It is something to be welcomed with open arms and is a simply glorious experience. I will never forget praying for Tessa, whose healing testimony I mentioned in chapter four. What I didn't mention is that she came

---

[39] Acts 10:44-48

back a week later on Zoom to ask for the baptism of the Holy Spirit. I agreed to her request and started to pray in tongues over her, asking for the Holy Spirit to come into the breakout room and baptise her. All of a sudden, it was like there was a wind all around her; her hair was blowing, and her arms were shaking with the force of the Holy Spirit for about five minutes. She was smiling from ear to ear. Hallelujah! It was a glorious sight to behold.

In August 2023, I booked to go down to a Christian worship event in Sussex which was happening during the weekend. Someone I know had mentioned that her son was not all well, to the extent that he was off work on sick pay. He lives near the conference I was going to, so I immediately offered to pray for him with my friend that I was travelling down with. Robin accepted, so we planned to go to his house on our way down on the Friday night. I had obviously never met him before, but I was dismayed to see a very fit young man who told us he was a shadow of his former self. He told us that he was suffering from dizzy spells, other neurological problems and ME like symptoms. Robin showed the three of us into his living room, and I immediately got a word of knowledge from the Lord, which was the word REPENT. I told Robin this was the word I had and asked him if he felt he had ever done anything in his life that he needed to repent of. Immediately he was touched by the Holy Spirit and was hit by a wave of contrition. He then started confessing and repenting of sins that he had committed when he was young. After that, we led him through a prayer of salvation and then we started praying for his healing. It was then that the Holy Spirit really showed up and Robin was absolutely blasted by the Holy Spirit from head to foot and started shaking all over so much so he couldn't stand up. We thought that we had just come to pray for healing, but the Holy Spirit had other ideas and Robin was baptised in the Holy Spirit for a good five to ten minutes with a big smile on his face. Jesus clearly has plans for Robin that we didn't know about and there is obviously a serious calling on his life. Robin was so overwhelmed by this experience that he wrote down his testimony, which he has very graciously agreed to share:-

"After many months of being very unwell within the last two years, my mother arranged for Victoria and Laura to come to my house and pray for healing for me. As the time approached for Victoria and Laura's visit, I started to warm to the idea of them coming to pray for me after seeing significant growth in my faith. I started to look forward to it. 19:45pm arrived, and I had just finished the last episode of 'The Chosen' season two, depicting the Sermon on the Mount. A car arrived on the drive, and I knew that it was time. I opened the door, welcomed Laura, Victoria and Ivan, and offered them something to drink and eat after their long journey. They refused and said they wanted to get straight to it. It was like they were here with a clear mission and wanted to start straight away.

They sat me down in the middle of the lounge and asked me about my symptoms and whether I was well before all of this, to which I replied that previously I had been fit, strong and in very good health. They were filled with compassion and love, and they said they were going to pray for me and that it might not be what I was used to and to relax. Victoria asked me if I had anything that I wanted to repent of, or if there was anything I had been struggling with. I had already been repenting for my sins, but I had felt over recent weeks that I needed to vocalise my repentance out loud, to truly let go and be totally set free. Victoria led me through the sinner's prayer. I did this and repented to Jesus out loud for the things I had done. At this point, I was immediately filled with emotion and burst into tears. I felt such unbelievable sorrow for what I had done, and I truly repented deeper than I had ever done before.

They put their hands on me at this point and started to pray for the spirit of sickness and infirmity that was over me to be lifted. They all started to speak in tongues (this was very new to me). All of a sudden, my right arm started to shake from side to side. Then, as they prayed, my whole body began to shake. They continued to pray, asking the spirit of sickness to come out in the name of Jesus. At this point, I was in my beanbag chair on the floor, and I hunched over forwards and started crying out. "Yes!" Laura said, "Put it all on the cross," instantly, my body stopped shaking and I lay back into my beanbag in one swift motion. I felt total peace. Ivan then said that he wanted to pray for the healing of my neurological symptoms. He put his hand on my head, followed by the others, and my arm started to shake again uncontrollably. My body was being pummelled by electric waves of energy again and again.

Finally, Victoria then asked if I was having problems with my heart. I had been having a lot of heart trouble over the last 6 weeks and was under medical care. They placed their hands on my chest and prayed for healing for my heart. I was smiling and felt amazing. I lay there breathing in and out, with an uncontrollable smile on my face. I was beaming from ear to ear, and I felt beautiful inside and loved. At the same time, I felt absolutely exhausted like I had just run a marathon, but it felt like a good type of tiredness. They anointed me with oil and told me that I had been baptised with the Holy Spirit. They all started to rejoice and cheer, playing music, which I loved.

What I didn't tell them before they started praying was that for the last 15 years, I had felt this strange, lingering darkness over my life that seemed to always follow me, wherever I went. It was a feeling of a kind of depression, though I had never been diagnosed with depression. I had committed some bad sins in my life that seemed to just accentuate this feeling. I rarely spoke of this with anybody but it was always a tangible feeling in the background. Occasionally I would feel a glimmer of joy and peace, every six months or so that reminded me of how I used to feel when I was a child.

They helped me up, and I was still in a state of disbelief at what had happened. My logical and inquisitive brain was trying to figure out what had happened and search for answers. I felt a peace and euphoria that was indescribable. We walked into the kitchen and I felt different. I felt exhausted, but I felt happy, I felt love and all the fear and anxiety were gone. I no longer have any fear of expressing my faith, and felt totally immersed in the Holy Spirit, and willing to do whatever God needed me to do, without reservation. I was now his. They told me that all of my sins had now been forgiven by Jesus. I did not need to hold onto them anymore. They were forgotten, and I could leave them behind. I was told to be strong in my faith and to lead a holy life from now on. I hugged them all, they said their goodbyes and then they left.

Although I could not explain scientifically what had happened, I knew in my heart that it was real, and had been the most powerful experience of my entire life and that I would be changed forever. Since that day, my life has never been the same. I have given my life back to Jesus and continue to serve him in any way in which he asks. I now have such compassion for those in need, a newfound ability to forgive, to be slow to anger and an indescribable love for everyone I meet. The relationships in my life, with family and friends that had been damaged by my anger and lack of forgiveness, have been completely healed. I now spend my time seeking out other people who are searching for God and teaching them to follow Christ. I feel so complete and all the darkness has gone."

Hallelujah! Glory to God! I have kept in touch with Robin since that day. He has told us his health has improved considerably since the summer. Now he is an on-fire disciple of Jesus, witnessing to many in his local prayer group and community. As I said, we thought we were going down just to pray for healing but the Holy Spirit had other ideas. Robin was fully immersed and baptised in the Holy Spirit that day, an experience that he will remember for the rest of his life.

Smith Wigglesworth wrote very eloquently about his experience of being baptised in the Holy Spirit, which seems to be rather similar to Robin's experience, 'She stood up and laid her hands on me, and the fire fell. There came a persistent knock at the door, and she had to go out. That was the best thing that could have happened, for I was alone with God. Then He gave me a revelation. Oh, it was wonderful! He showed me an empty cross and Jesus glorified. I do thank God that the cross is empty that Christ is no longer on the cross. Then I saw that God had purified me. I was conscious of the cleansing power of the precious blood of Jesus, and I cried out, "Clean! Clean! Clean!" I was filled with the joy of knowing that I had been cleansed. As I was extolling, glorifying and praising Him, I was speaking in tongues "as the Spirit gave me utterance". I knew then that I had received the real baptism in the Holy Spirit.'[40]

It is therefore, of the utmost importance to seek the baptism of water and the baptism of the Holy Spirit. I hope you can see how necessary it is as it gives us POWER when we pray for healing or deliverance for others. It is basically the difference between driving a mini or driving a Ferrari, and I know which one I would drive, (no pun intended by the way). I would not attempt to pray for healing or deliverance for anyone without it. It is crucial. I hope you can also see that Jesus is not just healing people today but he is still baptising them with his Holy Spirit as he did on the day of Pentecost. I believe that God is pouring his Holy Spirit out on mankind at present and we will see the lame walk, the sick healed, and miracles take place once more all over the world. This is prophesied in the book of Isaiah.[41] I believe this move of God is starting to take place now. Charlie Shamp wrote a powerful prophetic word in his blog Destiny Encounters in January 2024, which is illuminating, "I am raising up a generation of righteous warriors who will walk in the power and authority of my spirit. They shall be a beacon of light

---

[40] Smith Wigglesworth Devotional p.373
[41] Isaiah 59:19-20

in a dark world, shining with the righteousness that emanates from me. As you walk in righteousness, you shall witness my hand moving mightily in your midst... I am releasing a fresh anointing of righteousness upon you. It shall flow like a river washing away every stain of sin and unrighteousness. I am bringing forth a new wineskin, one that is crafted to contain the fire of the Holy Spirit. As you walk in righteousness, you shall witness the captives set free, the sick healed, and the lost saved. You shall be a vessel of my glory, carrying my presence within you wherever you go."

Chapter Seven

End Times

We shall soon be in a world in which a man may be howled down for saying that two plus two equals four, in which furious party cries will be raised against anybody who says that cows have horns, in which people will persecute the heresy of calling a triangle a three-sided figure.[42]

We seem to be living in an upside-down world now, one in which good is called evil and evil is called good. The Catholic church and some Protestant churches certainly seem to be pursuing an increasingly downward trajectory at the moment. Locking down the churches during the pandemic,

---

[42] GK Chesterton Illustrated London News 1926

although it might have saved lives in the short term, has been absolutely disastrous for the spiritual life of Great Britain. Many people felt abandoned by the church in their hour of need and have simply stopped going. It has also led to a rise in evil, the occult and witchcraft, which is no longer hidden but in plain sight now. A friend of mine recently went to a well-known London store for tea, and they were selling Lucifer biscuits on the menu! Books on the occult and witchcraft are sold openly in some bookshops now. What has happened to the good old-fashioned Christian values that I grew up with, which would not have tolerated such things? All of these are pointers that we are definitely living in the end times, and the war with Israel is a very important key to the puzzle.

As I mentioned at the beginning of this book, it mentions that a man will arise, a purported `man of peace' who will negotiate an end to the war in Israel, which has been raging since October 7 2023 due to all the appalling atrocities and killings that took place that day. The Jewish people right now are waiting for their Messiah to come and rescue them. Ten red heifers have been imported from America in order to be sacrificed for the consecration of the Third Temple which they are about to start building in Jerusalem. The altar has already been built for the temple incidentally, a special ceremony is going to be held by the Sanhedrin in which the altar will be consecrated this year and the heifers sacrificed. Those of us who have read our Bibles will know, however, that if any man arises claiming to be their Messiah before the battle of Armageddon takes place, he will be a FALSE Messiah because Jesus (the true Messiah) will not come back physically to earth until the end of the Great Tribulation which is believed to last for seven years. It will be someone altogether far more sinister! Orthodox Jews still refuse to recognise Jesus to this day, but a very prominent Rabbi called Yitzhak Kaduri knew the truth that Jesus is the one and only true Messiah, as he had a vision of Jesus shortly before he died on 28 January 2006. He left a note on his death revealing the name of the Messiah. The note read 'Yehoshua,' which is the Hebrew name for Jesus.

The Second Coming of Christ, when Jesus returns physically to earth, is at the end of the Great Tribulation to save Israel when she is alone and surrounded by all her enemies at the battle of Armageddon.[43] This will take place on the plain of Armageddon, which I visited a year ago; it is a huge

---

43 Matthew 25:29-30

valley that sits in the shadow of Mount Carmel. On that day, Jesus will return with all the armies of heaven. He will land on the Mount of Olives, which will split in two, and there will be a fierce battle to free Israel from all the nations that will come against her. This will be a glorious day when Jesus comes back, defeats his enemies, liberates the nation of Israel from all the nations coming against her, and peace will come to our world for a thousand years, but this will not happen before the end of the Great Tribulation and the battle of Armageddon has taken place. Israel is a very important time stamp in end times prophecy, and it certainly seems like we are at the point mentioned in the book of Daniel. I wonder if this purported `man of peace' will arise soon to bring an end to the war. It will be very interesting to see who finally does manage to broker peace and bring an end to the war!

Another thing that is happening in Israel at the moment is that many messianic ministries are springing up who are telling the Jewish people the gospel and they are realising for the first time that Jesus is the son of God and that he is the real Messiah. There is a real move of God happening in Israel at the moment, which is continuing even in the midst of war; Jesus has never stopped loving the Jewish people because he was Jewish, and he desires all of Israel to be saved. 'Replacement theology', which is the false belief that the church has replaced Israel in God's plan because they rejected Jesus two thousand years ago, could not be further from the truth. Jesus still loves the Jewish people, and the will of God is that ultimately, all of Israel will be saved.[44] We can certainly see that happening in Israel at the moment, where there is a massive outpouring of the Holy Spirit, even in the midst of war. I also learnt when I visited Israel in 2022 that there is a worldwide movement of Jews returning to their homeland. It is referred to as making `aliyah', which is also prophesised in the bible. We are literally living in a time when bible prophesy is being fulfilled in front of our eyes.

So how far away are we from the Great Tribulation and the millennial reign starting? Theologians have been debating this subject for hundreds of years, but I recently saw a timeline from one theologian[45] which stated that the world will be six thousand years old in 2030, which he believed marked the end of the Great Tribulation and the start of the Millennial Reign! It

---

[44] Romans 11:26-27
[45] Rock Island Books. The Berisheet Prophecy by C J Lovik

certainly feels like the world has been in tribulation for the last few years for obvious reasons because we have had a worldwide pandemic but we are not yet in the Great Tribulation. This will start when the trumpet sounds, signifying the Age of Grace has come to an end and that it is time for the rapture of the church to take place.[46] The word rapture is derived from the Greek word 'harpazo', which means caught up. On the day that the rapture happens all those who believe in Jesus and who have repented of their sins will be rescued and taken to heaven in the blink of an eye. It will happen very suddenly; those who have died in Christ will be taken to heaven first. Then, those who are alive will be transformed from corruption into incorruption, from mortality into immortality, to heavenly glorified bodies and taken to heaven.[47] Soon after, there is a great celebration in heaven called the marriage supper of the Lamb.

The rapture is one of the mysteries contained in the bible and for those who say it is an impossibility, there are two biblical precedents for this. Enoch was raptured to heaven, as was Elijah, and Elijah's swift departure to heaven was witnessed by his servant

---

[46] 1 Thessalonians 4:16-18
[47] 1 Corinthians 15:51-54

Elisha.[48] Elijah represents the living in Christ who will be taken up in the rapture, whilst Moses represents the dead in Christ who will be caught up as Moses died a natural death, unlike Elijah. This is evidenced in the Transfiguration when Moses and Elijah appear to Jesus on Mount Tabor. On that day Jesus, our bridegroom will come for us, his bride and there will be much rejoicing in heaven.

The marriage supper of the Lamb is also biblical. In the word of God, it says those who are called to the marriage supper of the Lamb are blessed, and we are described as the bride of Christ.[49] The rapture of the church is actually very similar to a Jewish wedding. In a Jewish wedding, the groom comes for his bride at an unknown hour, marries her and takes her to his house for the night. The next day, there are traditionally 7 days of wedding festivities. In the same way, Jesus will come for his bride on the day of the rapture; we are taken to heaven and celebrate at the marriage supper of the lamb. Interestingly, at the Last Supper Jesus says to his disciples he will not drink wine again until the Kingdom of God comes; this is believed to be a reference to the marriage supper of

[48] Genesis 5:24 and 2 Kings 2:11
[49] Revelation 19:7

the Lamb.[50] We are in heaven for 7 years and then return with Christ to fight against all the enemies of Israel during the battle of Armageddon. On the day he returns to save Israel it clearly says that Jesus comes back with all the heavenly armies.[51]

There is some controversy over the rapture of the church and the timing of it. Some Christians disagree with the concept of the rapture being pre-tribulation and say it is post-tribulation, whilst others believe it is pre-tribulation. John Derby preached widely on the concept of the pre-tribulation rapture in the 1830's. Some mistakenly think therefore, that it is a concept that originated in Victorian times as a result, but in actual fact, the rapture was a core belief in the early church. Irenaeus, who was born in AD 130 and an eyewitness to the apostle John wrote about it. Cyprian Bishop of Carthage, who died in AD 258, also wrote and taught the pre-tribulation rapture of the church in line with Paul's writings. The first direct reference to the rapture of the church is found in the early second-century writing of the Shepherd of Hermas. Describing his fourth vision, he says: -

"I saw another vision brethren – a representation

---

[50] Luke 22:17-19
[51] Revelation 19:14

of the tribulation that is to come."

Then in chapter 2, he says, "Lo! A virgin meets me, adorned as if she were proceeding from the bridal chamber," and "I knew from my former visions that this was the Church", and then "You have escaped from great tribulation on account of your faith, and because you did not doubt..."

Another point to consider is that the word church is not mentioned after chapter four in the Book of Revelation in the New Testament because we are not here anymore!

My own personal view is that Jesus is a loving and merciful God. He knows that the Great Tribulation will be a time of terrible war, famine and pestilence worldwide. So I believe that in his mercy, he will rescue the children and all believers in Christ on the day of the rapture. We don't know when that day will be, but we do know it will be a day of great gloom and darkness, a day of judgement, similar to the Day of the Lord, which is prophesied in the book of Joel.[52] It also says in the bible that we are not appointed to wrath and that Archangel Michael will rise up in the end times, and all those whose names are written in

---

[52] Joel 2:31-32

the Book of Life will be delivered, so in effect, the rapture will actually be pre-wrath.[53] It certainly feels like we have seen tribulation during the last few years but the church will be spared the wrath of God, which is during the Great Tribulation. His bride will be spared from having to go through the wrath of God. I was also given a scripture from the Holy Spirit on my last birthday, whose meaning is clear, that his bride will be spared from having to go through the Great Tribulation.[54] God has a time clock and we are nearing the end of the age of Grace. This does not mean the end of the world. It means the end of an age and the start of a different age, namely the Great Tribulation, which is believed to last for 7 years.

God has also been giving us signs in the heavens to confirm that we are living right in the end times. There has been a series of tetrads of blood moons this century in 2003-4 and 2014-15. On September 23rd 2017, there was a Revelation 12 sign when the sun was in Virgo, and the moon was under her feet. Nine stars from the constellation Leo and three planets, Mercury, Mars and Venus, appeared in perfect alignment above her head. Another very significant

---

53 1 Thessalonians 5:9
54 Malachi 3:17

sign in the heavens happened on 8 April 2024 when there was a total solar eclipse in the USA, making the letter A for Aleph; it went through 7 towns called Nineveh. During the last solar eclipse over America in 2017, it went through 7 towns called Salem! The two eclipses form a cross in the middle, which is the Hebrew letter Tav. It is the last letter in the alphabet and means truth. God is speaking. He is the Alpha and the Omega, the beginning and the end. Jesus himself said that there would be signs in the heavens to mark the end times and it says in the Old Testament that the moon will turn into blood and the sun darkened before the Day of the Lord.[55] This is all prophesied in the Bible, which is one of the reasons why Bibles are so hard to find these days! Not only that, but major flooding has been happening worldwide, devastating earthquakes, volcanoes erupting and rivers turning to blood. Earthquakes, volcanoes erupting, and rivers turning blood red are NOT caused by global warming. They are all end times signs from the Lord to wake us up. They are, in effect, the birth pangs of the Lord's return and are becoming more frequent every day. The river Euphrates has also dried up completely now, another prophetic sign. In the book of

---

[55] Matthew 24:29 and Joel 2:31

Revelation, it mentions the river Euphrates drying up to prepare the way for the 'Kings from the East'.[56] We are literally seeing biblical prophecy unfold in front of our eyes at a rate of knots now.

Jesus wants everyone to be rescued in the rapture of the church. If you are not a Christian, I believe there is little time left. It is vital that you repent and accept Jesus as your Lord and Savior without delay. We are at the door of the Great Tribulation starting. If you are in some kind of sin or backsliding, it is time to repent of that sin, turn back to Jesus, and amend your life. If you are a Christian, now is the time to prepare and to get yourselves ready and we can do that by praying daily, worshipping and being in the word; Jesus wants a personal relationship with each one of us; he doesn't want religion. Jesus is coming for a joyful, expectant bride, one that is worshipping often, not just in church. That is how to be a wise virgin and that is what we need to do in order to be ready; we need to have our oil lamps full daily, not empty like the foolish virgins.[57]

Finally, it is time for the church to ARISE, and

---

[56] Revelation 16:12
[57] Matthew 25:1-11

witness to our friends and family.[58] We can't expect the clergy to do it all, as many people have given up going to church because of the lockdowns of the last few years. There is a harvest that needs to be brought in, and it is a large one, so we need to shake of our apathy and get out there. It is time to know the authority we carry in Jesus Christ, walk in it, and pray for healing for the sick and the oppressed. If we do so, we will see healings and miracles take place in our nations once more. Finally, I would like to quote the words of Julie Whedbee given to her by Jesus for all of us which are rather beautiful, "Arise!! Arise my beloved, for your groom wishes to wed his bride! From before time was, I created you in my heart, and I knew you. Then I breathed life into you at your conception, and I caused a decree to go forth. This one is mine! This soul have I loved, and this soul is cherished and set apart, as beautiful and holy unto me. This soul will walk with me and commune with me, and enter into covenant with me through the sacrifice of my life and my shed blood. Because I rose again to new life, you will rise to new life! The old garments will be traded for fine new linens of righteousness, as they become garments of salvation.

---

[58] Isaiah 60:1-2

Your former sins that were as scarlet are made white as the snow, as you are washed with hyssop and perfected through obedience...My signs are everywhere. I have called and I have warned. I have given many, many opportunities for all to come to me. But you my beloved, have heard my cries for fellowship with me and intimacy, and have come to me. You will assist me in bringing in the larger harvest, and then your purpose will be fulfilled. The feast is prepared and many saints await you! You will sup with me, and there will be such celebration! There will be a homecoming that will exceed your utmost imagination, as we come together to usher in a new day!"[59]

---

[59] From www.iamcallingyounow.blogspot.com Sunday April 7 2024 Behold I come quickly and my reward is with me, to give to each man according to what he has done!

Image 1: The Valley of Armageddon

Image 2: Statue of Elijah at Mount Carmel

Image 3: River Dan

Image 4: Sculpture of Jesus at the Fountain of Tears

Image 5: Bronze statue of holocaust victim

Image 6: Bronze statue of Jesus embracing holocaust victim

Image 7: The Lion of Judah

Image 8: Horned Nubian Ibex at Ein Gedi

Image 9: The Dead Sea

Image 10: Mountains in the Negev desert

Image 11: Remains of column bearing the inscription Pilate

Image 12: Overlooking Jerusalem

Image 13: The Dead Sea Scrolls found at Qumran

Image 14: Paddling in the Sea of Galilee

Image 15: Under the walls of Jerusalem

Image 16: Gethsemane

Image 17: Garden of Gethsemane

Image 18: Entrance to the Garden Tomb

Image 19: Inside the tomb

Image 20: To God be the glory!

Milton Keynes UK
Ingram Content Group UK Ltd.
UKHW021851231024
450133UK00011B/658